STILLWATER

The Secret Life of Ponds

by

Wayne Snyder

Dedicated To Kids Of All Ages
With A Curious,
Inquisitive, Love Of Ponds

STILLWATER

Written and Illustrated by
Wayne Snyder

Copyright © Wayne E. Snyder, 2018

Some rights reserved.

Document Restrictions Summary:

Printing: Allowed for private use only
Copying: Not allowed. This document may not be copied or transmitted in any manner, in whole or in part, except for brief excerpts in critical reviews or articles.

CreateSpace Independent Publishing Platform
CreateSpace.com

ISBN: 978-1986815789

About Stillwater

Where there is water there is life. From the deepest oceans to the smallest puddles there is life abundant. The largest of these animals is the blue whale. The smallest is most probably not yet discovered.

Stillwater is an overview of just a few of the hundreds of life-forms that live in small bodies of water – in the quiet still-water realms of freshwater ponds. For in these very hidden locations can be found a hidden life.

Some pond animals are large and easily observable.

Animals like ducks, fish, turtles are all large enough to be easily observed so we won't go there.

Many pond creatures are very small. Some are what may be termed microscopic animals, or nearly so. And if you are patient, and look very closely, you will find some very amazing animals that can do incredible things you never, ever thought possible.

How does immortality grab you?

The benefits of small ponds to wildlife and people is not entirely understood. But we do know they are extremely important and, in fact, vital to all life on Earth.

The striking color illustrations are not only a pleasure to look at but will give you a sense of the extremely diverse forms pond creatures can take. The glossary of **Important Terms** will help you understand the language of pond biology.

In the hierarchy of biological classification I have focused mainly on the organism's **family**. Family is broader and further branches contain the organisms genus and species levels. Some self-study into biological classification and rank will help here.

Now let's take a closer look at the incredible secret life of ponds.

The Crustaceans

If you have ever eaten and enjoyed the unique flavor of a lobster, a crab, a prawn or a shrimp you have eaten a crustacean.

Like insects crustaceans have a hard exoskeleton, made mostly of a strong material known as chitin. For a crustacean to grow it must shed its exoskeleton when it outgrows it. That's called molting.

Most existing crustaceans are small but there are some monsters in the seas. The Japanese spider crab is the largest with a record measured leg span of 18 feet –

and, so far, the smallest is *Stygotantulus stocki* that measures a mere 0.004 inches – just slightly larger than the period at the end of this sentence.

Scuds
(Family Gammaridae)

This tiny freshwater shrimp is closely related to waterlice. It has a distinct head, a segmented exoskeleton, stalkless compound eyes and seven pairs of walking legs.

Scuds are benthic omnivores and will eat almost any organic material they find. Adults are easy to spot in a pond as they crawl on submersed leaves, twigs and bottom debris.

Incredible Fact #1 – Scuds have another common name: "side-swimmer". This is because it will swim backward on its side or even upside down.

Incredible Fact #2 – A scuds eggs develop, hatch and the young's first few molts take place while still inside the female's brood pouch. The young are released only when the female molts. When released they look almost exactly like small adults.

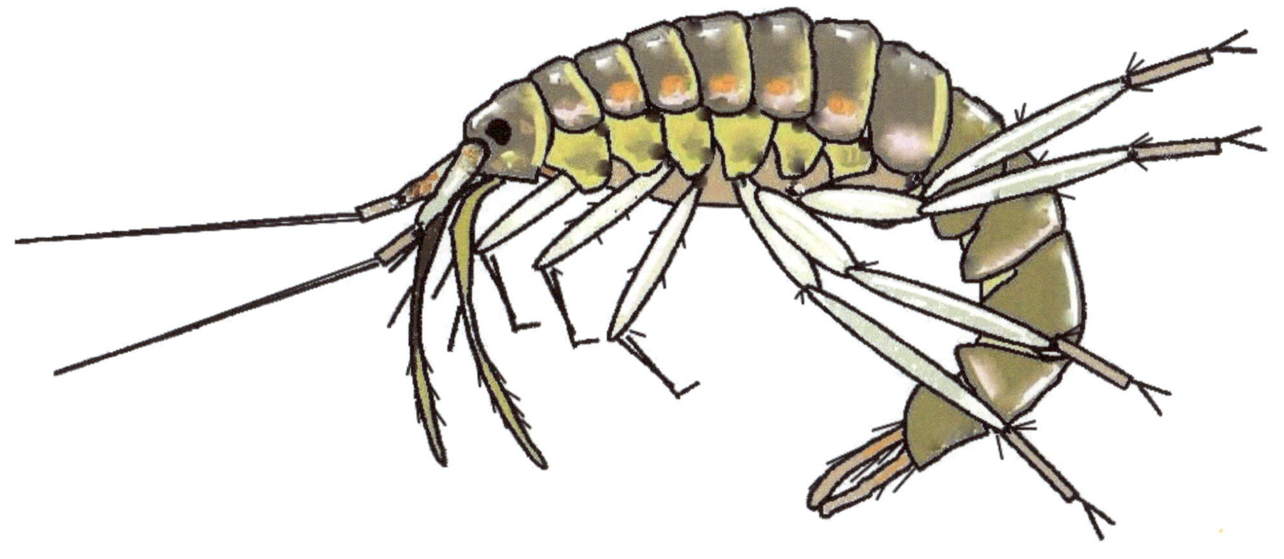

Adult Scud

Important Terms

Now that you have seen one example of how pond animals will be presented in this book, let's take a look at some important words (terms) that will help you understand them. Knowing the words and language of biology is important for understanding life on Earth.

NOTE: To help with understanding, some of the terms below are taken out of pure alphabetical listing and grouped into "Closely associated terms".

Adult – The final stage of life

Closely associated terms:

Larva (plural: larvae) – The young form of an animal which looks very different from the adult.

Pupa (plural: pupae) – The stage in the life of many insects between larva and adult.

Benthic – Living on the bottom of sea, lake, stream or pond bed.

Closely associated terms:

Littoral – Living on or along the shore.

Pelagic – Living above the bottom up to the surface of a sea, lake, stream or pond.

Carnivore – An organism that eats animal flesh only.

Closely associated terms:

Herbivore – An organism that eats plants only.

Omnivore – An organism that eats both plants and animals.

Decomposers – A group of organisms, largely bacteria, yeasts, and fungi that perform a function of breaking down dead organisms and their waste products into simpler substances.

Desiccation – Drying, pond drying.

Detritus – Silt, stones and organic debris formed from the decay of organisms.

Diapause – A form of developmental arrest in insects or other invertebrates during unfavorable environmental conditions. Diapause may occur in any life cycle stage including adults. Example: the eggs of some mosquito species will remain unharmed if they dry out, and hatch later when they are covered by water.

Diurnality – An animal that is active in the daytime is

said to be diurnal.

Closely associated terms:

Nocturnality – An animal that is active at night is said to be nocturnal.

Ecology – The study of relationships between living things and their environments.

Ecosystem – The interaction of groups of living organisms – plants and animals (the *biotic* component), together with their non-living or physical counterpart – soil, water, air, light, wind and temperature (the *abiotic* components).

Filter Feeder – A group of organisms that have developed a method of straining bacteria and other minute organisms suspended in water.

Limnology – The study of freshwater in lakes, swamps,

bogs, ponds and wetlands.

Morphology – The branch of biology that deals with the physical structure and forms of animals and plants.

Nekton (or nectonic) – Refers to organisms that actively swim in a body of water.
Closely associated terms:
Plankton (or planktonic) – Refers to organisms that are passively carried along by the current.

Obligate Species – Any organism that *must* use a vernal pond (temporary pond) for various parts of its life cycle.

Turbidity – A measure of the cloudiness of water.

Fairy Shrimp
(Family Branchinella)

This small freshwater shrimp appears to swim hanging "upside-down" as it filters food from the water. Adults have 20 body segments and 11 pairs of leaf-like swimming legs. Most species get no larger than 1 inch long.

Fairy shrimp swim slowly and are gracefully propelled by the rhythmic wave movements of their swimming legs.

Incredible Fact #1 – In harsh environmental

situations – severe and long-lasting droughts or frosts, hyper-saline conditions, complete dehydration, exposure to intense UV radiation – the eggs of this shrimp can enter a state of biological diapause where growth and metabolism are completely stopped.

These eggs can be revived from dormancy even hundreds of years later. Just add water and they begin to grow again!

Incredible Fact #2 – Some species of fairy shrimp have been known to hatch, grow to adult, produce eggs and die within a 15 day period.

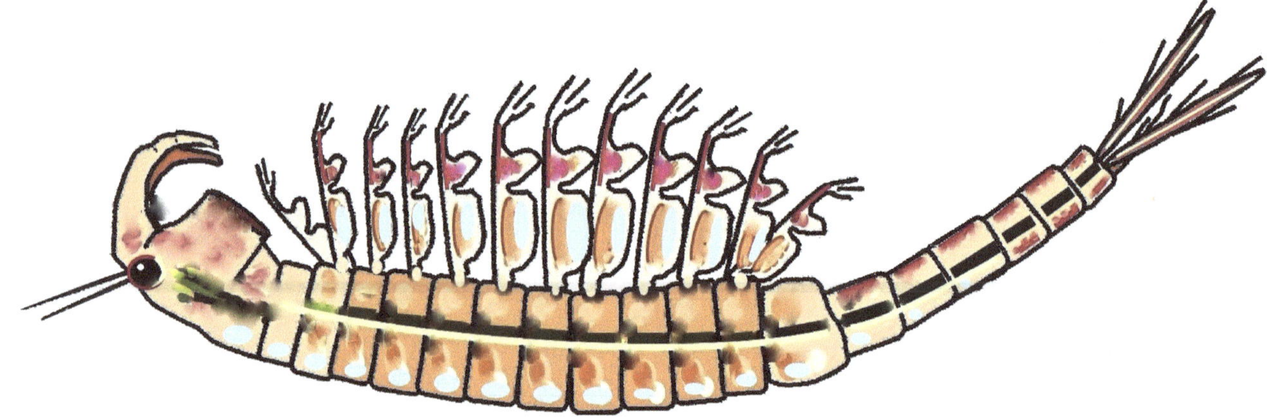

Adult Fairy Shrimp

Copepods
(Family Cyclopidae)

Members of Cyclopoida are feeble swimmers and usually described as planktonic critters living both in sea and freshwater. There is no shell and its body is divided into three portions: a combined head-thorax with swimming legs followed by four or five thoracic segments ending in a narrow abdomen with stiff bristles. Its head has a single eye which gives it the genus name Cyclops.

Incredible Fact #1 – Female copepods produce two

kinds of eggs; one kind that will develop quickly when habitat is favorable, a second kind when habitat is unfavorable.

Incredible Fact #2 – Some 13,000 species of copepods are known through-out the world so far. Some scientists say copepods form the largest animal biomass on Earth.

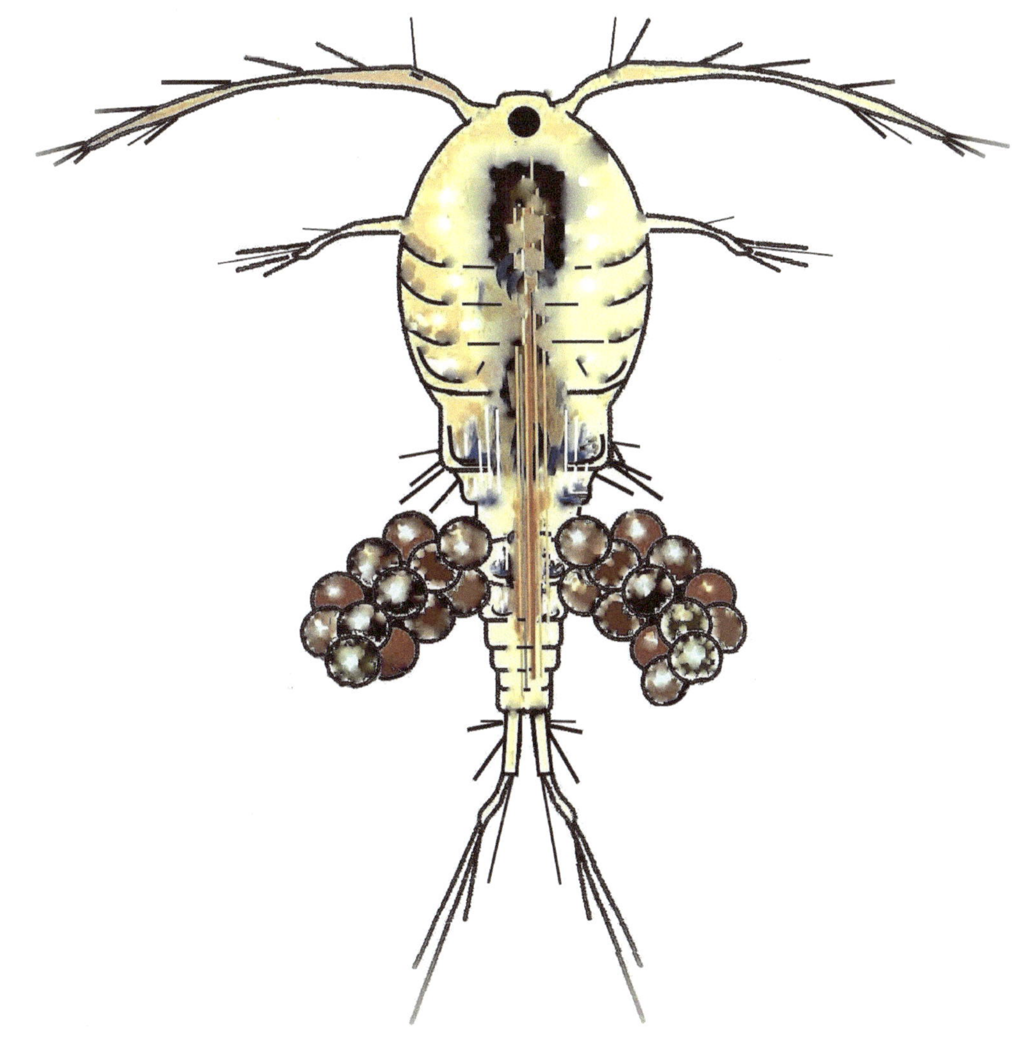

Adult Female Copepod (with eggs)

Waterfleas
(Family Daphniidae)

Except for its head this small animal's body is enclosed in a transparent shell only open on its ventral surface. Also commonly called daphnia, it has a single central eye and two pairs of antenna. The larger upper pair can be used for locomotion and give it the appearance of hopping through the water. They are pelagic filter feeders.

Incredible Fact #1 – Daphnia can produce hemoglobin in their blood to improve uptake of oxygen in poorly oxygenated water. When this occurs it may appear bright red.

Incredible Fact #2 – When they detect predators some species of daphnia can develop sharp spines at the lower end of the body and a helmet-like hood on the head to protect them.

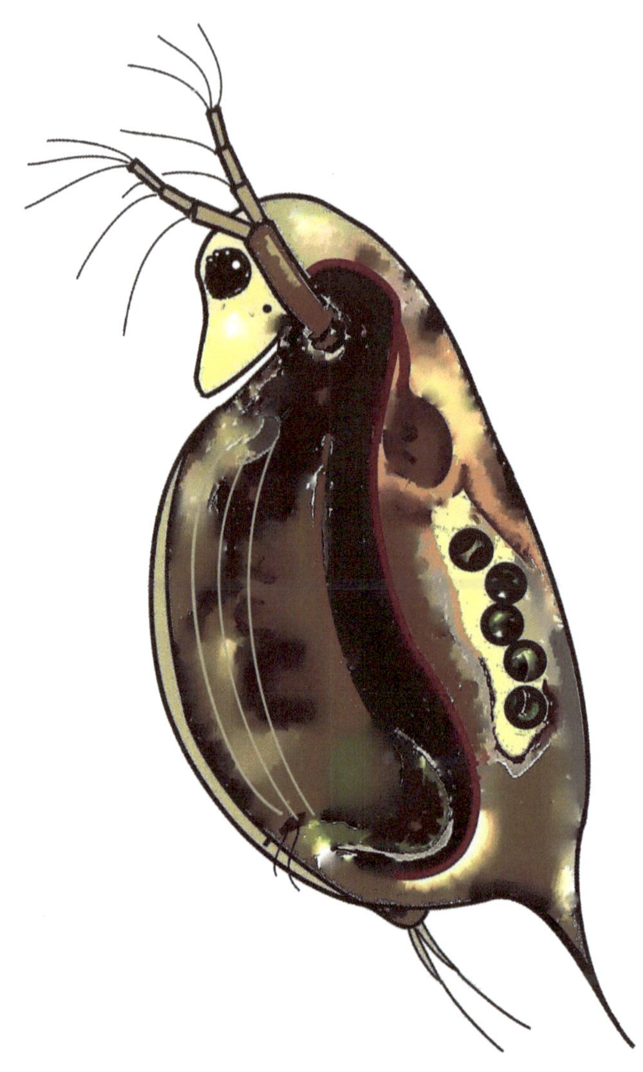

Adult Female Waterflea (with eggs)

Aquatic Sow Bugs
(Family Asellidae)

These animals are closely related to scuds except they are nearly flat. They are benthic and very secretive, hiding and feeding beneath submerged rocks, vegetation and other bottom debris. Like scuds they are omnivores.

Incredible Fact #1 – Aquatic sow bugs have a terrestrial (land living) cousin commonly called a pillbug or rolly polly because they are able to curl up into a ball when disturbed.

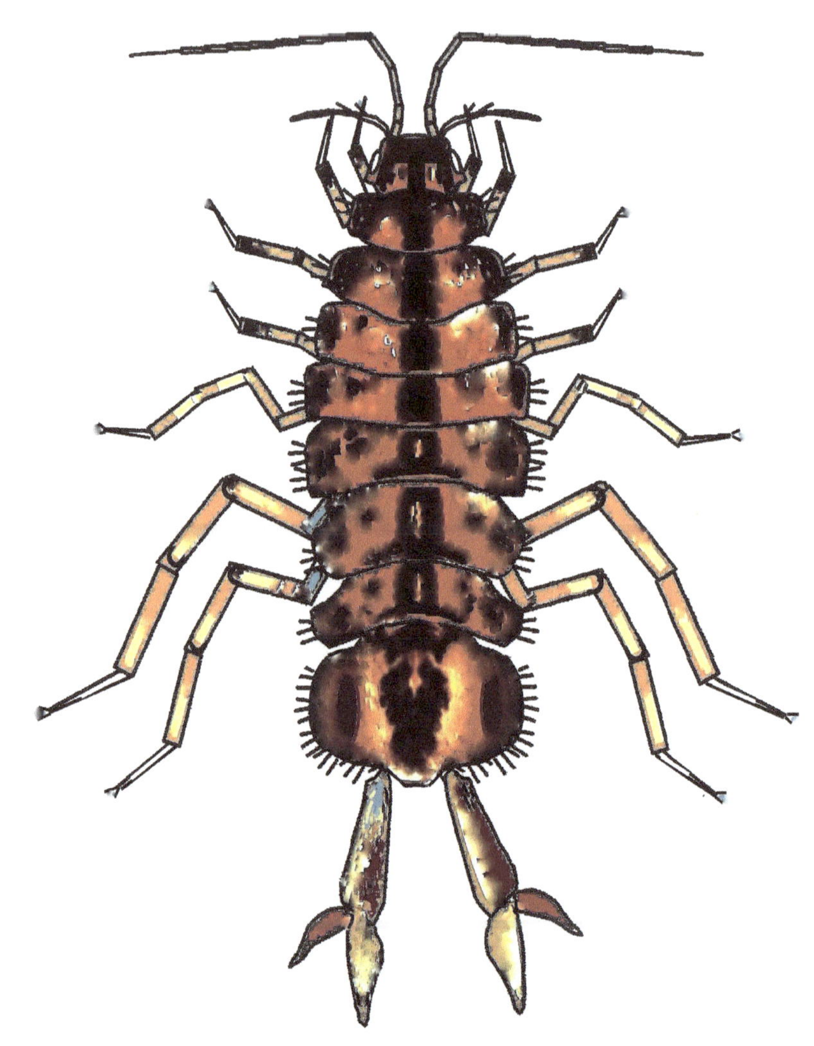

Adult Aquatic Sowbug

Seed Shrimps
(Family Cyprididae)

Seed shrimp look more like a clam than a crustacean. They live enclosed in an opaque, calcified, hinged carapace open only on the ventral side.

Incredible Fact #1 – Most seed shrimps have no heart or blood circulatory system.

Incredible Fact #2 – Some oceanic seed shrimp have an organ with which they can produce luminescent chemicals and if you capture lots of them can produce light bright enough to read by.

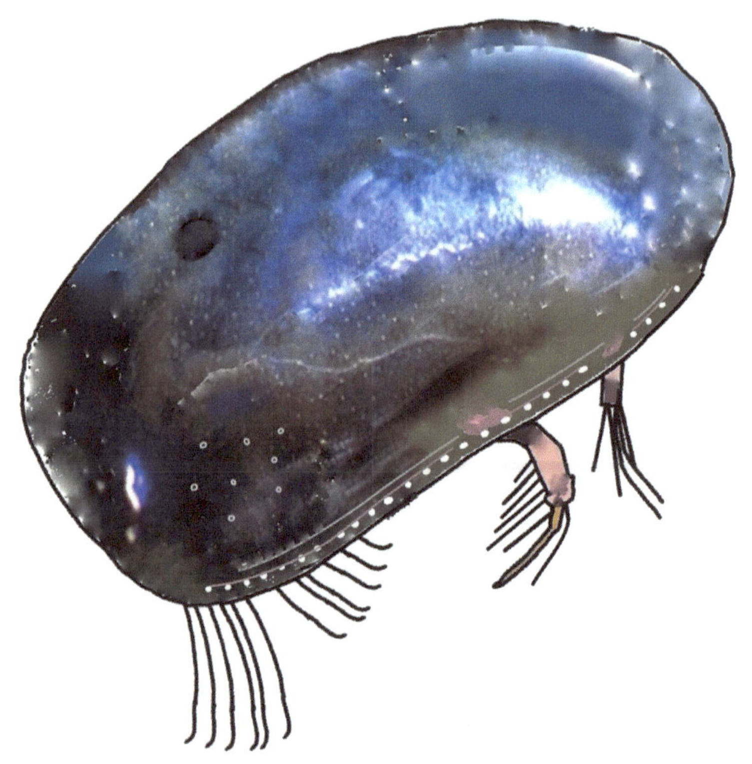

Adult Seed Shrimp

The Insects

Insects are found everywhere on our planet – in water, in soil, in wood, in the air – from the tundra to the tropics. Worldwide over a million different species have been identified with plenty more yet to be discovered.

This chapter will help you identify some of the more common and conspicuous insects that inhabit the secret world of ponds.

Diptera
(Family Culicidae)

Almost every human on Earth is familiar with the Mosquito. And most people know that it is only the adult female that "bites" and causes the irritating bump that can itch for days.

But few realize most adult females species lay their eggs in stillwater; that is – only in ponds. There, the eggs hatch and go through unbelievable transformations from larva to pupa to adult.

Incredible Fact #1 – Mosquito larvae must come to

the surface frequently to breath air and feed on algae, bacteria, and other microbes in the surface micro-layer. When disturbed they swim with jerky movements of their entire bodies, giving them the common name "wigglers" or "wrigglers".

Incredible Fact #2 – The mosquito pupa changes radically from the larva. The head and thorax present in the larva merge into a cephalothorax and the abdomen now curves around underneath giving it a comma-like body shape. The pupa can also swim by flipping its abdomen and it is commonly called a "tumbler". Tumblers do not feed at all.

Incredible Fact #3 – The eggs of some mosquito species remain unharmed if they dry out and hatch later when they are covered by water. Some species can overwinter as adults in diapause.

Mosquito Larva

Mosquito Pupa

Phantom Midge
(Family Chaoboridae)

Very much like the mosquito, the midge pupa changes radically from the larva. In fact the phantom midge will eventually develop into a winged insect that closely resembles a mosquito.

But while in pond water its larva hangs horizontally mainly due to two silvery air sacs at each end of the body. Although the illustration for the larva is grayish, its body is actually colorless and virtually transparent. It has two antennae and two black eyes on its head. It has a bristle-like "fin" at the end of its abdomen.

The head and thorax present in the larva merge into a cephalothorax in the pupa – now much darker - and the abdomen now curves around underneath giving it a comma-like body shape. The pupa develops breathing tubes that look like ears.

Incredible Fact #1 – Phantom midge larvae are carnivorous. Its antennae are really grasping organs with which they capture prey. This antennae impales and crushes its prey, then brings it to the larval mouth. They feed mostly on small insects such as mosquito larvae and crustaceans such as waterfleas.

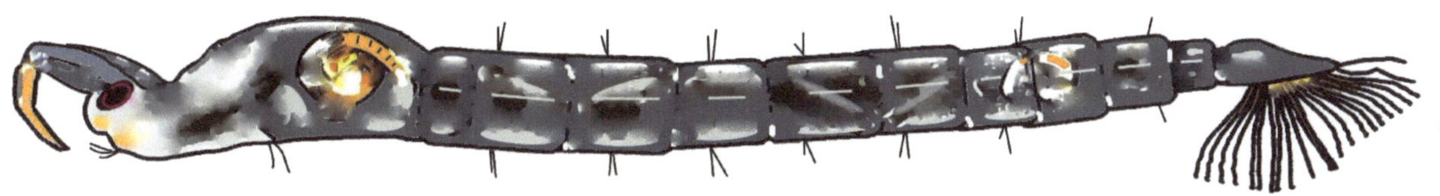

Phantom Midge Larva

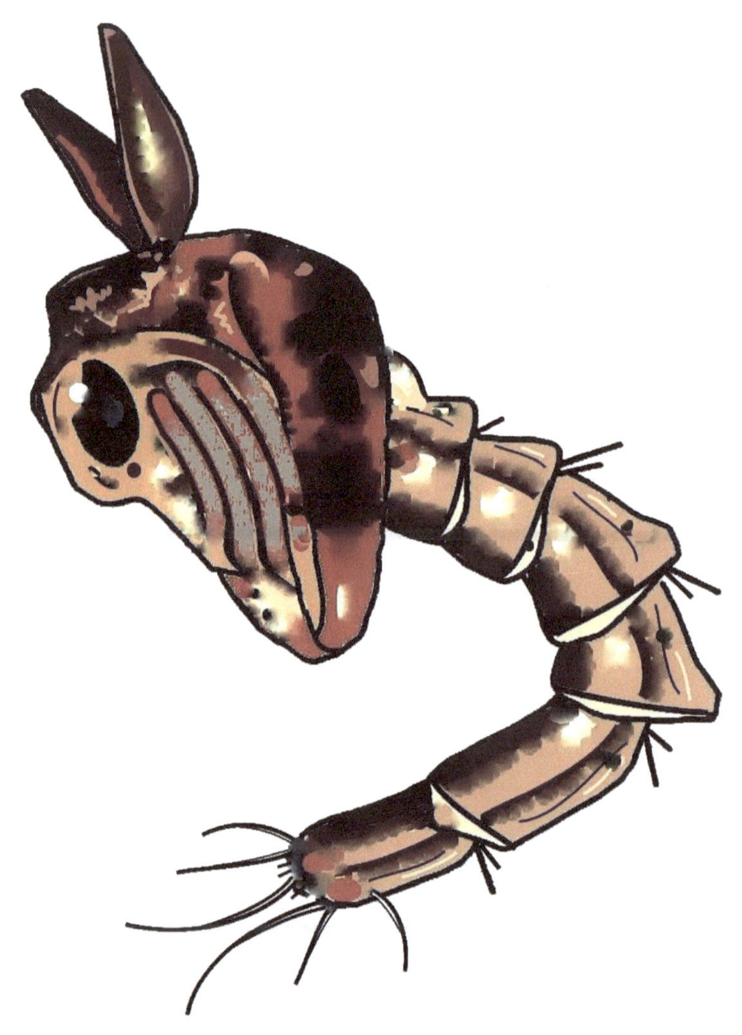

Phantom Midge Pupa

Crane Flies
(Family Chaoboridae)

If you compare the winged, spindly legged adult crane fly to its larva you will wonder how such a drastic transformation could occur. The larva is a fleshy, long worm-like creature with a small head embedded in its thorax. It has a pair of respiratory spiracles at its hind end surrounded by six fleshy retractile lobes.

Incredible Fact #1 – The fully developed larva crawls out of pond water and digs a tube-like chamber in damp soil. There the larva changes to a pupa and,

when ready, it pushes its way out of the soil as an adult
and flies away.

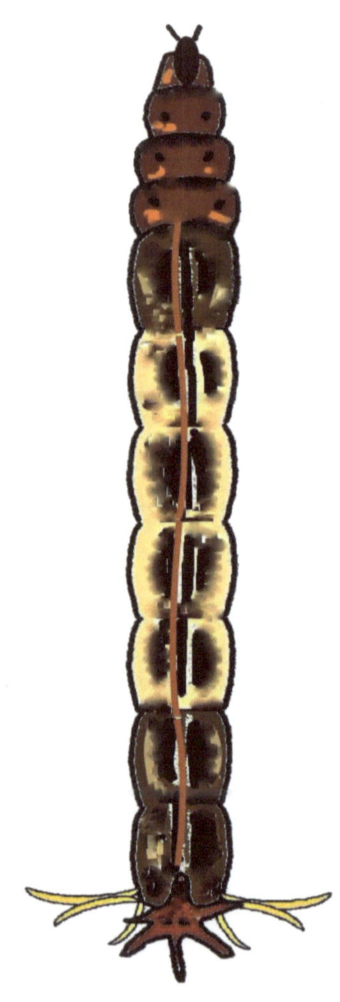

Crane Fly Larva

Predatory Diving Beetles
(Family Dytiscidae)

The two carnivorous beetles shown here – the **Large Diving Beetles** and the **Small Flat Diving Beetles** have a smooth, shiny, oval body. The hardened wing covers are usually grooved in the female and smooth in the male. Its long hind-legs are nearly flat and fringed with hairs which it flexes simultaneously like boat oars to get around. They have wings and are capable of flying from one pond to another at night. They feed mostly on mosquito larvae, water mites and other small pond insects.

Large Diving Beetles

Incredible Fact #1 – These beetles have sickle-shaped jaws and attack prey larger than themselves.

Adult Large Diving Beetle

Small Flat Diving Beetles

Incredible Fact #1 – Adult flat diving beetles can diapause in the underwater soil during dry parts of the year and winter.

Adult Small Flat Diving Beetle

Water Boatmen
(Family Corixidae)

The water boatmen has a long streamlined body with a broad head and large eyes. Its forelegs are short. Its slender middle legs are longer. But its outsized, hair fringed hind legs have the appearance of boat oars. Its abdomen is rounded and it has wings. Water boatmen are herbivores feeding on aquatic plants and algae.

Incredible Fact #1 – The water boatmen swims by rapid sidestrokes of its hind legs which give it a jerky, forward movement. It swims right-way up.

Incredible Fact #2 – It breathes air at the surface but can carry an air bubble underwater on its body surface or under its wings.

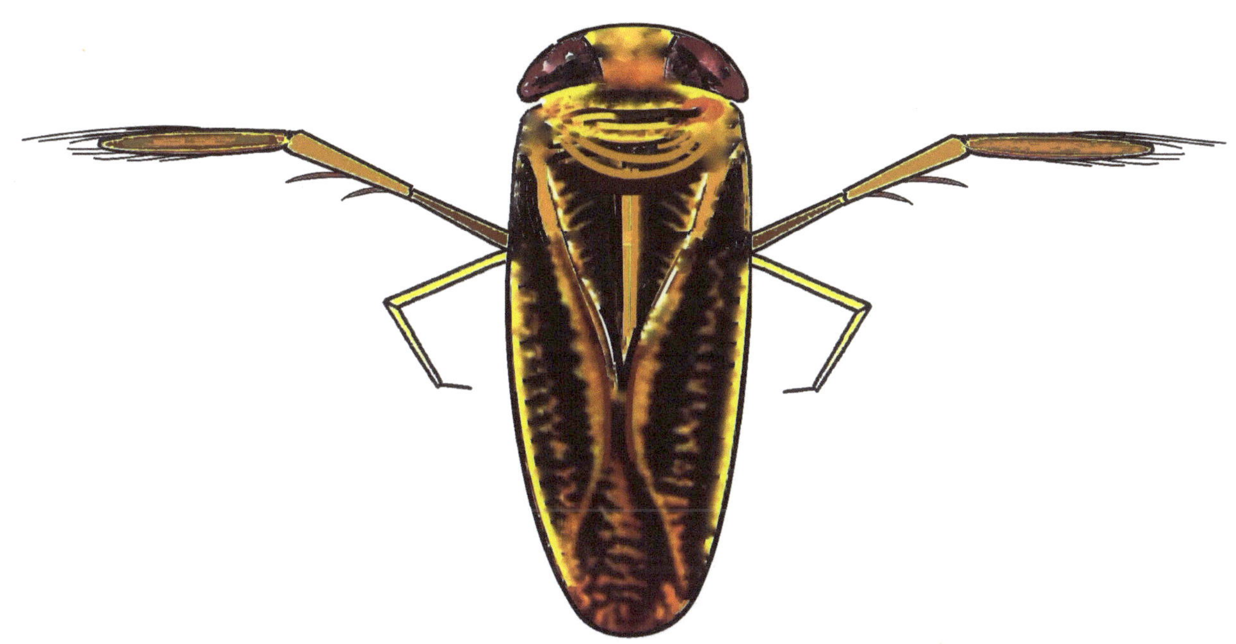

Adult Water Boatmen

Backswimmers
(Family Notonectidae)

Backswimmers look and behave similarly to water boatmen except for three important details – it swims on its back, it has no wings and it is very carnivorous.

Incredible Fact #1 – The backswimmer swims by rapid sidestrokes of its hind legs which give it a jerky, forward movement. It swims upside-down.

Incredible Fact #2 – It also breathes air at the surface but can carry an air bubble underwater held between bristle-like hairs on its ventral surface. If it stays inactive a backswimmer can remain underwater for up to 6 hours.

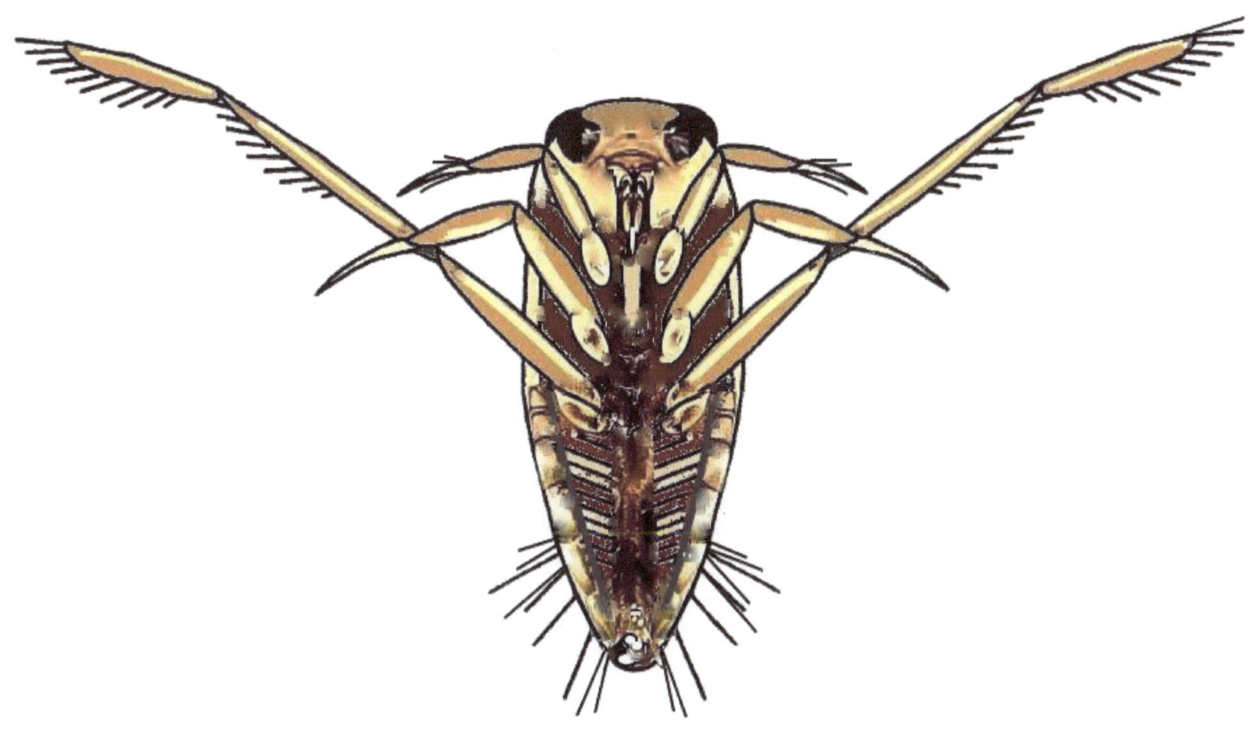

Adult Backswimmer

Freshwater Mites
(Family Hydrachnidia)

Mites are closely related to spiders and are found on land or in water. They are usually much more colorful some being green, yellow or bright red. Red freshwater mites are easily seen and, not fast swimmers, easily caught. For most mite species the nymphs and adults are carnivorous while others are herbivores.

Incredible Fact #1 – The larva of this red species of water mite is a parasite on the water boatmen.

Incredible Fact #2 – The bright colors of an adult water mite probably comes from the plants or algae it eats. The color might be used as a warning sign to predators. Just as likely its color is used to find or attract a mate.

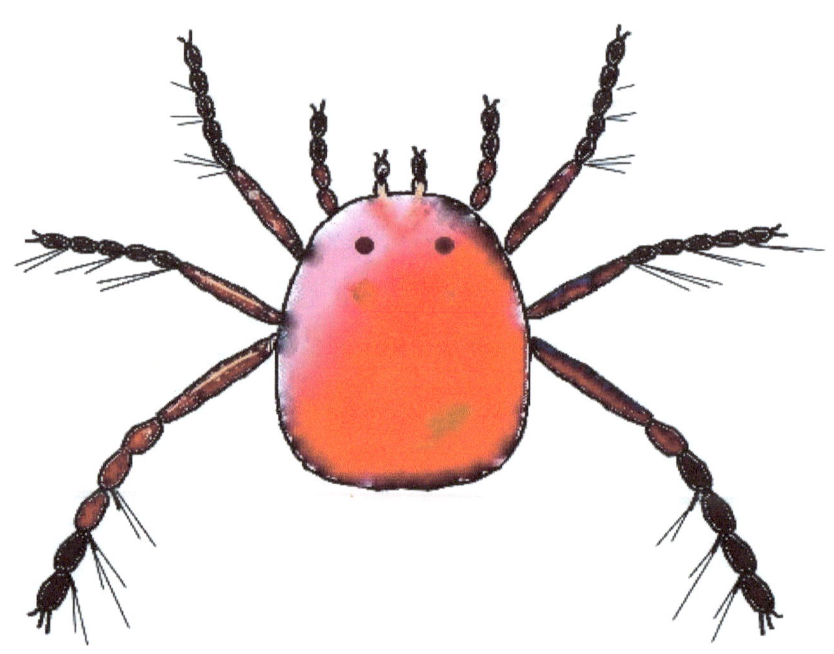

Adult Red Freshwater Mite

The Mollusks

Mollusca is an enormously large classification of invertebrate animals whose members are known as mollusks or molluscs. Mollusca includes slugs, snails, clams and other bivalve mussels, squids and octopuses. They have a soft, unsegmented body and most kinds have an external calcareous shell. As far as we know there are no squids or octopuses in freshwater ponds, but who knows, it's possible they haven't been found yet.

Freshwater Bivalve Mussels
(Order Unionoida)

Beneath this Order are dozens of Family and Superfamily species. Freshwater bivalves (mussels and clams) are characterized by a strong external, hinged dorsal shell to protect its internal organs. Like most bivalves, mussels have an organ called a foot which it uses to dig in the mud and get around.

Incredible Fact #1 – Freshwater mussels are some of the longest-living invertebrates in existence some with life-spans up to 200 years.

Incredible Fact #2 – Being filter feeders mussels in high population densities have the ability to improve water clarity.

Adult Mussel

The Planarian
(Family Planariidae)

The least amazing thing about this common pond flatworm is that it looks somewhat cross-eyed. Planarians move by beating small hair-like projections on its under-skin. This make them appear to glide along the pond bottom.

The planarian is mostly carnivorous eating both living and dead animals that they ingest in a mouth at the center of its body.

Incredible Fact #1 – Planaria exhibit the rare

ability to re-grow lost body parts. For example, a planarian cut lengthwise will regenerate into two separate but complete planarians. The same is true if cut crosswise.

Incredible Fact #2 – Planarians have excellent memories and can be trained to respond to stimulates. For example pairing a bright light with a mild electric shock will make it cringe.

Incredible Fact #3 – What's really incredible is if a trained planarian is cut in two and both halves regenerate into complete worms each half will develop the same light-shock reaction and will cringe.

The Planarian

The Leeches

(Family: Various families in the subclass Hirudinea)

Like its close cousins the tube-shaped earthworms, leeches are segmented worms but with flattened bodies. They are usually black or brown and some have attractive speckled or striped patterns. They are incredibly flexible and are able to expand and contract to the point where it's difficult to measure them. There is a sucker at each end of its body – one for feeding but both are used for getting around.

Common Pond Leech

Judging by all of the incredible facts listed here you might guess this is one amazing animal. It is. Read on.

Incredible Fact #1 – Leeches can move by "looping" like an inchworm or they can swim.

Incredible Fact #2 – Most pond leeches are parasites, equipped with sucker jaws that enable them to attach to the bodies of their hosts and consume blood.

Incredible Fact #3 – They can also secrete an enzyme that prevents the host's blood from clotting, as well as an anesthetic (pain killer), which prevents the host from noticing the "attack".

Incredible Fact #4 – Leeches, like their relatives the earthworms, are hermaphrodites, which means that each leech is both male and female.

Incredible Fact #5 – Large leeches can live for up to a year between blood feedings.

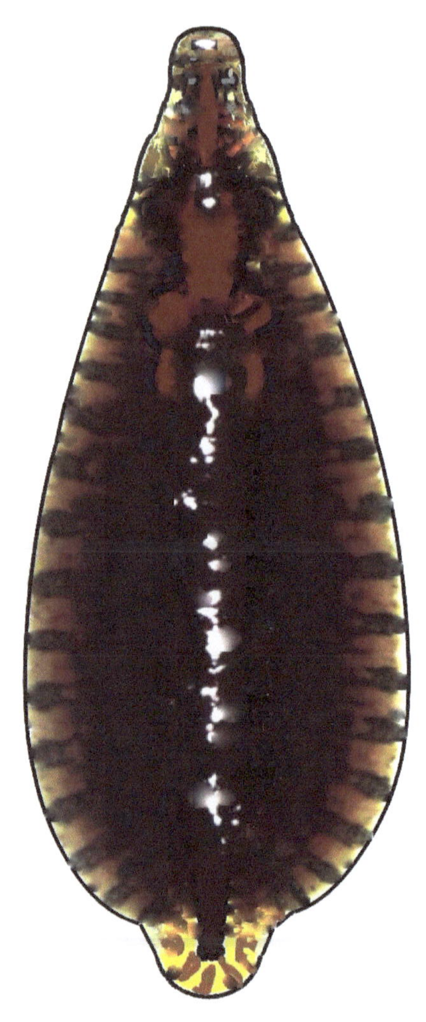

Adult Leech

The Hydra
(Family Hydridae)

The hydra is the most incredible of all pond animals. Its physical body is tubular with an upper mouth opening surrounded by one to twelve thin, moveable tentacles called cnidae. The tentacles are lined with stinging cells and can explosively inject a dart-like thread containing neurotoxins into its prey to paralyze it. Once its prey is immobilized the tentacles surround the animal and it is pulled into the hydra's mouth. Hydra feed mostly on aquatic crustaceans such as copepods and waterfleas.

Incredible Fact #1 – The hydra has a simple foot at the bottom of its body. Gland cells in the foot can secrete a sticky glue that it can use to attach itself to an underwater surface. A hydra can also slither along on its foot or completely detach itself and do somersaults to relocate itself.

Incredible Fact #2 – Research today appears to confirm that hydra have an unlimited life span – that is; hydra do not age and are, in fact, thought to be immortal. Also when a hydra is injured or a part of it is severed it will regenerate tissue and rebuild itself indefinitely.

The Hydra

For the Young Naturalist:

The Cecropia Moth (*Hyalophora cecropia*) is North America's largest native moth. It is a member of the Saturniidae family, or giant silk moths. Females can have a wingspan of six inches or more.